A Dog's Job of Work

ISBN: 979-8-9911983-7-0

Cover photo by Samuel Prestridge
Cover and book design by Alan Abrams

Sligo Creek Publishing Co.
Silver Spring, MD 20901

A Dog's Job of Work

Poems By

Samuel Prestridge

For my wife Jaqueline, my children Luke, Sarah, and Nathan;
for their beloved, Vale and Sam; and for my
granddaughters Elena and B.G.

All, without whom, not.

Finally, for Molly Hodges—before whom, shenanigans.

Contents

BOTTOM   Let me play the lion too. I will roar that I will
   do any man's heart good to hear me. I will roar that
   I will make the Duke say "Let him roar again. Let
   him roar again!"

QUINCE   An you should do it too terribly, you would
   fright the Duchess and the ladies that they would
   shriek, and that were enough to hang us all.

ALL   That would hang us, every mother's son.

BOTTOM   I grant you, friends, if you should fright the
   ladies out of their wits, they would have no more
   discretion but to hang us. But I will aggravate my
   voice so that I will roar you as gently as any sucking
   dove. I will roar you an 'twere any nightingale.

   ~A Midsummer Night's Dream, Act I, Scene 2

Prologue: How to Tell a Story

Jesus the South is fine, isn't it. It's better than the theater, isn't it. It's better than Ben Hur, isn't it. No wonder you have to come away and then, isn't it.

~Absalom, Absalom

Unravel it,
slowly, but tautly, the last strands
of rope, turning, turning,
slowly separating
as the hero scuttles over the burning bridge,
the starlet in his arms. Then,
let everything crash down.

Say, *in 1933, a farmer with a lot of kids—*
specifics and details—*19 kids, all sons
to strap and carry, all deaf, all look-alikes,
planned Christmas on a cotton bale,
his last, and him with a large family—*

"Large family": this needn't be mentioned again
because it says, implicitly, how old
the man must be, the kids too,
which is integral to the story:

*They were old enough to have their own minds—
not mean, but knowing
just enough to ruin Christmas.*

He'd meant to swap the bale for gifts
and couldn't have them with him.
This, too, is implicit: "old enough
to have their own minds"
demonstrates the value of the idiom,
succinct, a brightening of salt,
adding authenticity.

By problem and solution, let the plot develop.

*He'd gotten up that morning
before the kids awoke . . .*

1

This being a farm, that would be, say, 4:00 a.m.:

. . . the wife up, too, cold breakfast, cold stars outside,
the bale already loaded, and the hand-cranked, flat-bed truck
waiting to be started.

The participle will infer that something's pending,
and the situation will create itself—will offer details
to unpack, tangential, but unavoidable:
"hand-cranked" denotes the setting of the spark,
tinkering with magnetos, and the danger
of the crank kicking back, breaking your arm for you.
All that done, he'd be ready.

He tried to crank the sullen truck, and WHAM!

(A useful interjection, "wham"—)

. . . the crank kicked back and broke his arm.

Now, we forget Christmas and the bale,
everything but pain and the urgency
to crank that truck.

So he set the spark again . . . .

Here, pause.

They'll suspect what's coming, but won't believe.

Then WHAM!

And understatement:

He couldn't even raise his arms
to wipe tears from his eyes.

This may seem an ending,
but you can't just leave it there—
him, hopping around the yard, his arms twin trout,
Christmas pending, the kids asleep.

What happens next is toe-nailing,
a carpenter's effect. The story takes off
at an angle, but one thing leads to the next:

So the wife woke up the oldest,
the dumb one, who could drive the truck.

The boy took out the spark plugs,
put them on the hearth to warm.
He siphoned gas into a syrup bucket . . .

(again, details authenticate—)

took off the breather, put gas in the carburetor . . . .

A cat jumped to the fender while he held the breather,
rubbed against the syrup bucket, sloshing gasoline.
The boy got mad, ran the cat.

Here, quicken the pace.

The cat hid under a white pine stump.

They'll think they know what's next.

He doused it with gasoline . . .

Here, the reader winces.

and struck a match

Here, say Whoosh!

For the denouement, talk slowly.

Be deliberate.

The fire-cat ran across the yard,
setting it on fire,
across the cotton bale,
setting it on fire,

into the barn where goats were kept,
setting it on fire.
And everything burned—
even the goats—
and the boy stood looking dumb
and the farmer, arms broken,
couldn't even beat him,
and Christmas was potatoes, buried in the yard.

Next, tie the story off,
relate your own life to it:

The boy grew up to be the guard
at the Fox Run city dump,
the image of his father.

To close, insist it's true.
That father told father, and you got told.
If there must be a moral,
let it always be the same:

God works in wondrous ways.

Now:

Part 1: Mississippi Half-Steps

A Poem for Uncle Jackass (October 27, 1927 – August 14, 2016) Written, Mostly, while Standing Up in His Hand-Carved Pirogue, a Hammer and a Bag of Nails Hanging from My Waist, Nailing Up the Last of His Gospel Signs--All According to Codicil

They must think I'm dancing on the water
as they come around the bend of the river
and see my jerky moonwalk
as the dead man's pirogue dry humps backwards.

   Between blows of the hammer, I hear them
on party barges, laughing, grilling fat
burgers, talking girls out of their swimsuits
for the vitamin D in sunlight.
   They follow the signs to where I'm tethered,
standing in his pirogue, hammering his last
hand-painted, neon, apocalyptic screeds
to boney, gray cypress knees, buttress roots:

--And I will come in hot judgment . . .

 And witness against sorcerers . . .

And against the adulterers . . .

And against all false swearers . . .

And against oppressors, saith the Lord.

His hatreds were infectious. Even buried,
he remains, a spasm, a spirochete
in my brain, blood, my spinal memory.

   Nailing up his signs, I live his meanness,
and I'll stay to watch the letters weather,
to watch them vandalized to splinters
for firewood or for spite.
             I'll hear shooters
tuning pistols dotting *i*'s, pinging
a's, e'*s*, and *o*'s, hollowing the pristine
letters of his mandates, as his strictures

true my hammer.   No keening strikes, careening
nails--ricochets to blind an eye.

                              His anger's
in the balance I lose as I hammer,
in my knees, locked against the rocking pirogue.
In my stance, my stiffened back and arms.

In my labored breath. In my vertigo.

Reception
(for Karen Salyer McElmurray)

In that part of Mississippi, radios gave up
long, blond howls on Sundays.
God's voice, a double-sifted ghost
drifted through bad gospel groups,
sports news, and always, always settled
on the shows whose hosts sold miracles
and secrets of the chosen.

When Heaven seemed a done deal,
the earth would shrug, and we were lost
as before, lost and arguing
which way to turn the dial.

Raised thus for partial measures, folks grew
to shout down what they had no use for,
learned to raze opinions
on Sunday afternoons so calm their voices carried
sulfur to wherever I had fled, creek, barn, or pasture.

I hear them yet, the old ones, still arguing
short fallings, what the sky held back,
the heart of them, holy, pure,
and just beyond reception.

Early Morning, Driving in a Spring Rain, through Shuqualak & Headed toward Meridian, Mississippi, I Think of the Miserable Death of David Ruffin

On either side, fences swallowed
in green, the rusted barbs subdued
a purple moment. In chiseling rain,
a field, a sodden mule, one foot
cocked in nasty patience, as if
he'd gotten old in that bogged spot,
waiting for someone to kick.

Driving since dawn and nerve-shot,
I wish up "Ain't Too Proud To Beg"
for its back-beat like a gray mule's hope,
how green and sympathetic,
the live wires hum for hearing
I know you're going to leave me,
but I refuse to let you go . . . .

He must have learned to sing in church,
the bluesy gospel jumps defying belief,
the sweet slides down as if falling were landing.
Against a voice like that, such rain!
The wet fence shimmers like a chance to lie.
The gray mule calculates the odds
of ever getting even, and still attends.

Loose Gravel

1.
Then, a ten-year fugue state, fever running
the same patched road, shattered
tons of any elsewhere
tarred and graded to continuum,
leading only to Hattiesburg
                              and another
dress rehearsal for giving up a son.

2.
Six a.m., a bypass near the city of my birth,
taking a curve at sixty. Then,
born for such collisions,
a loopy, fluttering Little Sulphur
jittered, hovered over the blacktop
for the sudden *Ping!* and shivering
of car antenna.
                  Six a.m.
and in rearview, a pirouetting, butter-
pat-shaped fumbling, *Eurema lisa*,
bookmark in the passing lane.

3.
If love is a trust and
trust is in relation,
one comes to such by scant
half inches, by a word
made flesh and locally
peculiar.
              Odd moments,
stupidly luminous,
sort themselves to tether,
or mime a tethering--
a splay of wrenches spaced
equidistant on a workbench
moored in concrete.
    Morning follows the arc,
shines one chrome wrench each hour
    A mechanic I know
keeps his time this way, keeps

the where and when of him.

4.
Near Brooksville, in stopping
for breakfast, I posit no gods
but ones we make, which is not
suggesting they aren't waiting
for us & putting on big shoes.
    A baker keeps her shop
here, a Mennonite whose
god's a quirky sort, hating
chrome, but blessing her scones,
fritters, her jellyrolls,
sticky buns, her bear claws,
and butterfly pastries.
    For him, she's faithfully
painted kitchen fixtures
black. For him, she wears her hair
in buns, butter-yellow
twists, whorls that praise his name
and market her pastries.

She grudges my being
in her shop. It's her way
of taking my order,
eyes downcast, serving me
the same, eyes clenching tight,
I swear it, whenever
she tops off my coffee.

As devotion, revulsion
are the same in the dark,
I wildly tip her talents,
two bucks on a five
dollar tab, enough to help
her buy another can
of aerosol black paint,
should her graceless god feel
some small, personal slight.

5.
Lunch anywhere, if I stopped,

(Shuqualak, Scooba, Toomsuba), would be dire
apostasy of Grab & Run fast foods,
arrays of over-done fried
chicken, odd burritos shaped
like parcels from a psychopath, spiced
potatoes, rolled in meal and tossed
in hot deep-fat. In narrow aisles, racked
cartons of candies and snack cakes named
for sounds that no one otherwise makes—*Ding
Dongs*, *Ho-Hos*—as if merit resides
in cloying nonsense, as if I could
buy a *Koo-Koo* and not feel unmanned
in the kingdom of road-food
that fattens, never feeds.

6.
Leaving, I'd hope to smell like fried chicken,
walking through air violet with chicken-
scented smoke that settles a patina
of chicken on everything in town.
   I can nose a civic history, sniffing chicken –
scented hair products, chicken-scented canned
goods, chicken-scented stomach remedies
costing more than sandwiches, chicken
scented greeting cards, chicken-scented toys
for chicken-scented kids, chicken-scented
motor oil for trucks, cars on which the scent
of chicken settles, the chicken-scented
magazines with naked women who smell,
it's imagined, as nothing ever smelled
and upon whom men can speculate their
technical whethers and hows while choking
chicken-scented chickens, chicken-scented
playing cards for killing chicken-scented
time, and condoms, rainbow hued and chicken
scented for a numbing rounce beneath a
chicken-scented moon *under which she lay*
cane fire all around her hair eyes ashen
already pulling me down hold still now
she said we got time and me already
thinking somewhere else and leaning backwards.

7.
Pass it all at sixty!
Better no time, like the present
cool, numbed cruise and fumble, radio fixed
on somewhere up or down the road. And, yet,
in passing, Citizen, note the junkyard,
the rows of washers, dryers, ovens ranked
and shining as they can in whatever sun
the earth will spin, the odd gaps—panels,
doors sold for salvage—sprayed with jonquils.
From the mouths of dead appliances, a sunburst
feigning sunlight. Even speeding through,
I caught the jonquils wagging
their temporal sass while lifting,
lifting themselves from the blank, ruined mix.
Out of the rusty darkness, such yellow.

In a Sudden Downpour at a Poorly Planned Blues Festival, the Ghost of Robert Johnson Comes upon a Dumpy Guy Sitting in the Rain on a Wooden Crate & Eating a Soggy Spare Rib Sandwich (for Luke, my eldest son)

He returns as a catch in the bass man's stammer,
the drummer's septic pulse, returns
from wherever he listened, cold and alone.
Anyone hungry knows--he'd swap hermetic precision
for our bad weathers. He'd envy the rainfall
our muggy huddlings, envy mud
the imprint of our asses.
                              How would he not
aspire to be even the oddest of us?   How would he not

assume for a sogged conveyance
that dumpy man riding out the storm, eating
a dripping sparerib sandwich
& watching a skinny woman, dancing in the rain.

> *Soaked and undulant,*
> *Crown Royal bottle her faulty umbrella,*
> *she is shaking out her bones, shaking*
> *out her demons, while black clouds laugh,*
> *laugh thunder down upon his wanting*
> *her, laugh as she drops the bottle,*
> *gallops down the slope to disappear*
> *in muddy green & rain & swelter & sound & crowd,*
> *to swallow it all, chaser to her whiskey.*

Ghost, you'd love her as the dumpy man
must love her, who tugs in half the sandwich to point
the way of her passage, who mops the rain
& sauce & sweat before he bites the other half,
who grins the gap as if to ask you,
Who else could be as lucky?

Just as a Huge Tree Falls into the Headwaters of the Mississippi and Begins Its Drift Southward, an Underwater Welder Talks to me about Diving, Zero Visibility, and the Threat Imposed by Neutral Buoyancy (Greenville, Mississippi)

After his wife left, fled, or went back home to give birth,
decided not to come back, and didn't send word
of any issue, he never spoke of her, the child,
never tried to see the child, avoided anyone
who might ask.
                 I sometimes thought of the kid, soaking up
whatever his mama's people might say, soaking up
whatever anger might be brought to bear in meeting,
refusing to meet the father.
                 After she left, he spent spare time
in the pool, testing diving gear. He liked to see his shimmering,
breath, where bubbles hit or missed pretty girls swimming by.

"You breathe," he said. "Whatever else is just convergence."

If that's so, I said, why stay here?   She's left. You've stayed put.

Said back, "Big money diving in the Mississippi.
At depth, you can't see anything, water's so muddy.
That kind of dark, you just work and breathe."
                 What worried him:
"A tree falls in the river, soaks two thousand miles.
It soaks and sinks up until it doesn't sink or soak.
Just heaves along, keeping whatever depth, toward the Gulf.
A 1,000 pound trunk will soak up 2.5 times
its weight, gets here moving along at three miles an hour—
fifteen-hundred joules of force, time it gets to me."

Said, "Do the math. Won't see it coming. You stop waiting
to die, go on with your welding. Hope it's the next guy's
look-to. If he's lucky, he'll never know what hit him."

After an Impossibly Steep Hill in Yazoo City, through Three Stoplights, Past where Wu Hor's Grocery Use to Be, then over the Humped-Up Railroad Crossing . . .

the Delta begins, and the land's so flat you'll see rubber miles
past whatever you sight. You'll come to believe you've grown taller
than anything this side of the horizon, less and except
road signs, bridges, historical markers—impediments made
by someone like you . . . which only makes you taller still, taller
than trees edging fields, allowances made by someone like you.
And you're taller still—so tall you stand flat-footed, step across
the Yazoo, Big Black, Yockanookany, Sunflower rivers,
the bayous Goshen & Choctaw. (Passing, dip a toe in each . . .
just to say you did.) You're tall enough to straddle fields, to watch
crop dusters buzzing your ankles, to gauge disappearances,
the slow evaporations of Tchula, Midnight, Panther Burn,
Drew, Alligator, Itta Bena, Ruleville.   Impossibly tall
now, you breathe the halo-drift, the dust from known and unknown
graves--Robert Johnson, Jack Owens, Elmore James, R.L. Burnside.
You draw conclusions. Taller than any arbiter, you stride
west to Rosedale, where the river has receded,
                                        and you stand
on the Mississippi River's bank.
                        You're so tall, you likely
can jump it with a running start; you're tall enough to wade it
with impunity, to feel the prehistoric cold sucking
both your feet into a muck for which there is no referent.
Stand there long enough, the river may return, may take the ground
beneath your feet, however tall you've gotten. It plays no role
in casual assumptions, will not be bound by any faith.
The Mississippi plots shenanigans, keeps insouciant
counsel, biding time, planning outrage. The river does not choose.
It goes its way, redefining scrabbled bedforms, leaving
oxbows, cutbanks, point bars, fields of national mud where nothing
wise grows.
            Size yourself against the mudflat between the river

and a withering town, notable only in Johnson's blues
for being on the riverside . . . which it isn't anymore.
Wait there until dusk. The sunset makes the Mississippi shine.
What were your expectations? What did you hope in coming here?

Villanelle: Mourning the Death of Ray Charles, but Thinking, Actually, of Blind Willie Johnson

Sadder than Ray's first night in the ground,
the knuckle bones of dead men, the archive of their sounds,
their ways of saying *lost* and *waiting to be found*.

The honeyed slide guitar, the frayed voice, graveyard bound,
growling the gospel, and a hard rain falling down.
Sadder than Ray's first night in the ground,

his "Dark Was the Night" and "The Soul of a Man." No sound
this side of "I Got a Woman, Way Cross Town"
like "Nobody's Fault but Mine." However found--

--stoner cousin's vinyl or hippie shops downtown--
the day is darkly lucky when I hung around
(sadder than Ray's first night in the ground)

to hear his howling *ne plus ultra*, to propound
blue moves for doing something like, snuffling to hound
his ways of saying *lost* and *waiting to be found*.

Since then, not much to tell. Protracted rounds
of whiskey cut with ditch water. A shrug. A slipping down.
Sadder than Ray's first night in the ground,
confusing getting lost with waiting to be found.

When a Woman's Finally Had Enough in Alligator, Mississippi, She Walks Down Highway 61 to 444, Doglegs to Highway One, Turns South, and Walks to Rosedale

Land so flat, you can watch her
walk for three days straight—you can
watch her put mad feet to ground
she wants behind her (no plan
but slapping roads hot & straight
as hell's by laws), plodding
twenty-six miles in a heat
to match her anger, no ride
or rider either. She means
by this to say *You're left.*

Except:

you can sight her between thumb,
index, pinch back when she's down
to size. Hold her. Pocket her
to keep the small voice piping
hot. Rest of your life: *Who knew
what went wrong,* she'll shrill.
You'll do nothing but listen,
sag in a heat for keeping
scorpions, her being a
boil on all your possibles,
a burning you'll husband till
you limp in dotty circles.

Or:

You can watch her feet, her legs
disappear in heat shimmer,
blue-white radiance: she'll look
hip deep in split milk, juking,
dancing her own jubilee.
Lean forward in your chair.
Think how there's music—must be—
places she's walking. Think how
you might hear what makes her move
that way, if you were closer.

Part 2: Work Songs, Refusals, & What We Got Is Idiom

Poem in Which My Father Turns into Ten-Pound Boxes of Bulk Pork Sausage (after a Wrong Turn while Driving a Truck for My Father, Hattiesburg, MS)

Coming out an alley, an old woman
is cursing her pig. Must be: unswearing,
no one fidgets hands that way, flopped sneakers
mopping up what she'd not want written down,
white-hot syllables sizzling the concrete.

He's mute beneath the beatings, his ass broad
enough for her broomstick hiding, his back
sloughing vile Anglo-Saxon invective
as he trots toward home for supper, crossing
casually just in front of my truck

as I wait idling, trots past my truckload
of waxy boxes--loins, butts, sausage (bulk,
patties, smoked), chops, shoulders, hams. My father
would know the current market price for each,
the waste, hours, equipage, hands, costs to cure

him into product, (offal flushed or drummed
for dog food). He'd know the calls to be made,
scheduling to keep the roads hot, accounts
receivable, salesmen's swarm and yammer,
accounts payable, gabble of jobbers.

I don't know if he'd see the joke here, but
I know what he'd think of burning his dime
to watch her beat him home, wondering why
she curses him for being who he is
& having places to go, orders to fill.

Lucretius, Spitballing, Writes *Nothing Comes from Nothing*, Takes a Break

He grins, slaps the top of his desk, leans back, thinks how no one's
said *anything* like this, *ever.* Thinks *Well . . . then . . . it's not true,*
strikes it twice through. Writing since dawn, he fusses his pens,
makes a *to-do* list, stares out the window, across his land.

In a rented lot, the miller's son goads a drowsing mule
hitched to the wooden shaft turning the granite runner stone.
He steps back, fumbling his pants, turns to pee on the heaped grist.
The miller stops tending the hopper, crosses, beats the whelp,

then lashes the mule, which has stopped its plod to graze dried grass
beside the packed clay path. The startled mule lopes a circuit,
plods, stops. The miller hauls the grist to rinse. The boy, weeping,
picks up the goad and slashes the air, walks over to sit

on the charred stump of the tree under which he was conceived.
The miller cut it down and tried to burn the still green stump,
thinking his wife unfaithful, swearing he couldn't be sire
to such an idiot. He'd beat her if he could care, still,

but he can't anymore. Lucretius knows them both, requires
no proof of her fidelity, but misses the tree's shade.
Paternity is patent in the idiot, for nothing comes from nothing.
He reconsiders the stricken line, then writes STET beside.

He watches the boy wipe his eyes, struggle to stop his weeping,
as he grabs a flail, limps toward the drowsing mule. He smashes
its sleepy face to see the mule gallop the barren ground.
The boy slashes with the flail as the mule races faster

until the runner stone jumps free, shattering the bed stone,
wrenching the shaft assembly loose. Mace head and spindle trail
behind the disappearing mule. The miller abandons
rinsing, screams the boy transparent, slapping, raging until

he's spent, and sits on the clay, swearing, his head in his hands.
The mill is wrecked, and the mule is grazing in a hated
neighbor's wheat, forecasting a fist-fight by dusk. His business
had been good, piss-sodden wheat notwithstanding. He'd held gray

hopes, another mule, another mill. Now, there's no redress
but finding the boy to help him salvage parts, separate
millstone shards from the flour, and bag what all's redeemable.
But the boy's fled to the woods. He'll stay there until supper

or until the wife goes out to fetch him. *Maybe she'll seek,*
out while there, Lucretius thinks, *devil's*
helmet, belladonna berries for the miller's breakfast—
an omelet, with relish, to pay him for all he . . . never

did. Lucretius swears and double strikes through STET . . . .
If he lives, Lucretius thinks, the miller will come and ask
to borrow money. *Months in arrears on rent, and he'll ask*
me for a loan. Without it, he can't rebuild, can't catch up

on rent. I refuse, and he packs up, steals off in the dark.
If I do, I'm pouring piss down a rat's hole, but nothing
given, nothing gained . . . He wants to smash his inkwell. Instead,
he takes a breath, a fresh page, tells himself *Yeah . . . what the hell . . . .*

I'll keep it. What's the worst that could happen? It's just a poem.
He places a fresh page on his desk as a servant comes,
bringing bread still hot from the oven, fresh milk, and honey
just robbed from his hives. Lucretius tears and bites the bread,

grinds down on a particle of grit.

Seven Guys All Wearing Reflective Gear and Hard Hats Have Taken a Break from Trenching a Sewer Line, and They're Standing in a Row and Looking Straight Up into the Trees, Maybe at the Cross Arm of an Old Wooden Power Pole

Whatever aligns them is lost,
lost in the welter— branches, limbs,
quilting leaf-shadow.
                        Whatever
arrests their attention will be
nothing specific to their jobs.

I know by the red mile of ditch
they've dug—and having dug will fill—
by rows of stacked concrete culverts,
by the backhoe's idling rumble,
pillow talk of post-coital trolls.

It's not my job. It's not my line
of sight, so I can't say.
                        But
driving, I've watched a power line's
splice box morph into a perched hawk;
a hawk on a line pole's cross arm
turn into an insulator.
I've seen odd shapes sustain, deflate
hopes—it's why, I think, they're staring
upward, imagining a hawk's
burden, his weighty algebra:
x mice times y acres over
z blacksnakes to the nth power,
an equation solved with a sweep
of his wings.
                        Here, they'll just bury
their best efforts. Here, completion
will equal extinction: no one
flushing, washing will recall
their work, and their children, decades
on, will exhume and replace them
with another red mile.
                        Maybe

24

the men are thinking this. It's why
they're taking a beat and staring,
hoping it's a hawk. It's a way
of imagining dominion.

Funereal Geometry: The Evangelical Congregation Concludes the Funeral by Singing "In Christ, There is No East or West / No North or South," while Outside the Church and Midway Up, a Steeplejack Tests to See the Steeple's True

If a plumbline's run from Heaven's door bell
to the red baize on Satan's pool table;
and if such a line bisects their steeple;
and if the steeple's perpendicular—

perpendicular, foursquare, ever true--
to the church's temporal foundation,
the workman's spirit level always rules
theology *and* recalibration.

Lacking such, the skewed will keep on skewing,
will mime secular drift–anathema
to the faith and the faithful, those who cleave
to the steeple's cleft, crowd a receding

circumference, and create a holy
right angle to the vertical axis.
That's why the steeplejack's climbed the steeple
even as the funeral rumbles, smacks

around his calibrations. He's allowed
no room for error in the elders' view:
the journeyman's warrant is the last word
in church doctrine. The steeple must be true,

must aim straight up. The soul shoots for a pole
implied by the steeple. Off-plumb slivers
of a bubble, who knows where the launched soul
might end up. Heaven's the point of a pin.

As We Withdrew from Afghanistan, I Remembered the Canada Geese at Fredericksburg Battlefield Park

1.
By the war's 18th year, we'd as well lost
ability to grieve for silent names
scrolling up the TV screen each evening.
They're just babies, my wife would say. Sometimes,
we'd talk about who was going to hell
for starting this. We became insensate
to suffering, to people blown apart
while praying, to young men needing to be
told why they fought. It wasn't apparent,
and the rationale kept changing. I wrote
letters to politicos, snarky screeds
in local magazines. I was looking
for something, a toehold, and remembered
a gaggle of Canada geese, last spring,
browsing a weedy football field, moving
from the fifty, five yards one way, five yards
back, foraging for grubs and greenery.

2.
I followed, pretended to explain how
each webbed step
                      could stencil Burnside's pacing
vacillation, his waiting here three weeks
and watching Lee's army fortifying
Marye's Heights across the river. Three weeks
fidgeting to cross the Rappahannock.
The eve of battle, he saw no reason
to change his plan: build six pontoon bridges,
trundle 60,000 soldiers across
in plain sight of an acre of Rebel
sharpshooters, storm Marye's Heights, thrash Jackson,
Lee, march on to take Richmond, end the war.

He'd tried the same at Antietam, three times,
marching soldiers under sharpshooters' fire,
across a stone bridge. Five hundred men lost,
three hours shot; then, the Rebels withdrew,
and he learned nothing to carry forward.
Three weeks vacillating, watching Lee dig
and fortify the Heights, and still he wrote,

*I think now that the enemy will be more surprised by a crossing immediately in
our front than in any other parts of the river . . . . We hope to succeed.*

Two days' fighting saw Lee still on the heights,
Burnside retreating. Twelve thousand Union
soldiers lost, three thousand Confederate,
and the town destroyed.
                    From the Heights, Lee said,

It is well that war is so terrible. Otherwise we should grow too fond of it.

There are those I'd like to see it carved on.

3.
Across the road, kids playing soccer,
a riot of running, yelling, kicking
the ball the wrong way, while dads pace sidelines
and moms mill about, slice chilled oranges.
I crossed the river, stood at the stone wall
at the foot of Marye's Heights. Sharpshooters
here, lined up four deep, fired, went to the back
of the line, reloaded, pacing forward
for another shot at the Yankees, bunched
in clumps, ragged ranks, but marching forward.

Now, behind the wall, a young girl sorted
candle pallets, bales of white paper bags
for a yearly remembrance. *It is well,*
said Lee. I guess I thought so, too. I asked her
if I could take her picture, and she smiled.

Say Antietam, I said.
                    She'd never heard
the word, but tried to say it, just to please.

Behind her, crosses, hundreds, chalk white, nameless,
aligned across the golf-course-green hillside.
Scouts, Cubs, and Brownies placed white paper bags
graveside, and parents following would drop
white candles in each.
                    They lit them at dusk
for swirling, loopy, dotted lines of light
and, less distinct, penumbra of headstones.

Aviators, passing, might well wonder
what they're trying to spell.

Leavening

A chorus of suicides, old relations worn out
by marching in place, a whining off an icy bridge,
three ODs . . . no, four. Four: the dead pile up since I'm not
done, not done rasping them faceless, not quite done amid
this shifting about, this clattering, good bones grated,
ground, sifted for a tone-deaf daily bread.

ESOL

Then,
Jesus was a cousin gone for smokes.
We listened, and his '66 Mustang
sank beneath the crickets.
                        Against the quiet
someone told how, down the road, a woman
dropped dead, just dropped dead--her kids pulling out
of the drive, Sunday dinner plates greasy,
unstacked—dropped dead by the coffee table,
eyes open, still, and staring three hot days
through the coffee table glass--three hot days
of a Mississippi August, three days,
wilting and dead carnations declining,
their mottled pinks and whites, to kiss her eyes,
the ghosts of Mother's Day.
                        Then someone else,
I wonder what that woman did for God
to punish her like that.
                        We didn't know,
wouldn't guess, did steadfastly nothing, but
wait for Jesus's grumbling engine.

Getting a Haircut from the Only Woman in Monroe County, Mississippi, Who Was Willing to Go to Funeral Homes in the Middle of the Night and Style the Hair of Corpses

My scalp listened, her fingers' telling
phone calls, 3 a.m., when the corpses
were prepped. She'd wash and dress their hair–
mom's silvered pixie, granny's blue helmet–
turn death into a Sunday nap,
so visitors would walk softly, whisper
what they'd left to say.
                            Wash, rinse, wash, rinse.
She styled by pictures left for her
and aimed for open-casket—
no surprises, but covering surprises.
A gunshot to the temple might untoward
the familiar, might demand a nightmare
comb-over; facial cruelties--slashes,
crushed cheekbones--might be concealed
by a Nora's luxurious swoops,
cascading locks.

I thought how the dead missed out
on what her fingers said, the warmth
of her body on the back of my neck,
a flesh scent, almost floral, I'd recognize today.

She told me she was never scared.
Indifferent to the opinions of the dead
or just not superstitious, I didn't know.
I never asked if she talked to them
the way she talked to me--if she passed on gossip,
secrets, the way she'd pack a lunch.

I simply asked if she saw it as a sideline or a calling.
"The dead are only customers," she said
and leaned me back to rinse my hair.

What We Got Is Idiom
(In memory of Don Wrighton)

Because anybody can see and hear and smell and feel and taste what he expected to hear and see and smell and hear and taste and wont nothing much notice your presence nor miss your lack. So maybe when you can see and feel and smell and hear and taste what you never expected to and hadn't even imagined until that moment, maybe that's why Old Moster picked you out to be one of the ones to be alive.

~*The Mansion*, William Faulkner

1.
Driving from Oxford
there are words I say
evoked by land
pulp-wooders skinned—
fallen trees,
unused, ghostly
even in noonlight,
houses, abandoned
for no reason I can tell
but everybody ends
up going somewhere.
There are words—to say
them is to summon
images that pull
nowhere
but backwards.

2.
East of Pontotoc,
a dump truck blocking traffic
and the scraping of machinery.
The road's sloped shoulders are shaved
to a stubble of gravel and red clay,
overhanging pines cut back,
branches strewn road-side,
then ground into an aromatic mulch
that's sprayed to staunch washed-out ditches.

Stores here petal
with parked cars—those working the road,
those who've come to watch
the wrecking and repair
as though it were something to buy.

The dust, terrific, drifts
through miles of limp barbed wire.
Even the land is leaving.

3.
Last night,
I told a story from Vermont,
how a woman said I'm lucky
to be from Mississippi:
Such an ignorant . . .
backward . . .
violent . . .
place . . . .

You must have lots to write about.

I just thanked her, I said,
as I realized
I was dealing
with an idiot.

A listening woman stood, yelled at me:
That's wrong . . . that's . . . that's just not fay-uh!
the undulant, slick syllables,
setting what her Daddy said
against a slow erosion,
worse repair.

4.
There was a man who screamed
at disembodied voices, and nights,
he snored lulled threat.
For years, his voice, sand grinding a lens.
Nothing settled, so he was lobotomized.
There, his doctors said,
charged the state and waited

as he mumbled at his stitches
grew louder, almost wheedling
as the voices whispered, now,
sighed, a cat's back brushing lightly,
as he hushed back,
demure, subdued, but persistent
*What? If you'd just . . . . A little
louder . . . . I didn't
quite . . . . What?*

5.
The stories that we tell,
draglines through the dark,
chants for and against the night.

The reprieve is connection
to tradition,
which is an aspect
of memory,
which is a part
of romance . . .

which is *marketable*,
and a downhill grade to hell
where Cerberus,
wise-assed, unconvinced,
has three heads:
one to snap you coming,
one for leaving,
and one for while you stand
and think *Now what?*

He can be bought with cakes
the legends say, or if you're musical,
the rhythms of a song
will make him sleep,
and you can go in to see the dead,
and maybe even leave.

The dead, for all your efforts,
still knock together;
the dog, asleep, is still as monstrous

as your tune, its last notes,
fastens to the rocks,
a lichen,
a clam.

Everybody's got a story . . . .

6.
My uncle said:

His dog went, too, as was natural for dog & John Haines both,
when John's mama sent him to the store. John's daddy was a
sharecropper, it was planting time, and the grocer was a good man,
mostly, giving credit to the farmers who had no money, much, until
the crops came in.

The grocer kept accounts, of sorts, of what each owed, and they
settled up at harvest to the dime.

The system worked and hinged on the good will of the grocer; then
all at once upon the appetite of John Haines's dog, who loped into
the grocer's, braced forepaws on a cracker barrel's rim, and started
wolfing crackers.

John watched, and the grocer watched, kicked him when John
didn't.

Then both watched the dog roll, scramble up, and run yelping out
the door.

John Haines grew pensive. *D —d-don't you . . . know,* he asked the
grocer—John, he was bad to stutter—*d-d-don't you know y'ought n-not
k-k-kick m'd-dog? Y'ought never kick m'dog.*

Don't you k-know I got to whip you now?

36

And he did and for a long time, and people stopped to watch.

The grocer, too, was occupied, dodging, keeping track of things
John beat him with to charge back to his family's account: plow
lines, one horse collar, a slab of salt pork, one new boot, and a jar of
horehound candy John took with him.

John's mama tried to make the grocer understand.

He said he did, and then, he cut their credit.

The time before John Haines left home was measured best by
groceries.

Leaving, John stopped to tell the grocer this, who with business in
his cellar, had the doors locked, didn't hear John knock.

John Haines left a note & home, came back in a year, a traveling
comedian with a jake-leg, one-truck vaudeville show, as befits a man
with too honed a sense of justice.

That was John Haines.

7.
You see? my uncle said.
*The sun don't shine
on one dog's ass all day.*

8.
I am speaking a dead language
that has taught me to want
the things I walk away from.

9.
The dump truck clears the road,
and a flagman waves me on. The column
starts behind the pilot,

skims through the repairs and rearrangements
as I think of a woman who told me
Leave things where you found them
so they can keep their power.

To be located by more
than what I'm moving through . . . .

This morning's sun deflects
off the last pane intact
of a house that's been abandoned.

The pilot car is leading me
through clouds of dust and light.

Part 3: Push Pins for Astral Projections

Husbandry

He's burned his yard, his garden.
Across the char, he's sown lengths
of razor wire, shattered glass.
He considers the scatter
every morning, over eggs,
coffee, NPR; shovels
salt to fill his burlap bag,
its faults mended--the fabric,
a grandma begging to die.
He washes dishes, vacuums
spilled salt, throws the devil some,
throws over his right shoulder
a loop of worn rope. He drags
the hundredweight heft of salt
into the black yard, drags it,
all day long, over scattered
glass, razor wire. After work,
he turns on sprinklers, watches
from his porch, the salt-water
runnels.   He allows himself
one mad whiskey and takes stock,
thinks about his neighbor's yard.

He does this every day--nights,
he plans the next. He believes
he's writing his testament
in Arabesques, geoglyphs,
pantomimes of crop circles,
loopy nods to finger prints.
He draws spinal memories.
He believes someone's watching,
someone whose name he's trying
to spell, someone huge beyond
all pleasing. She will rise up,
incandescent, from the salt
when, in lucky ignorance,
he spells it right. When he sees
her, she will irradiate
his labors and will walk so
her feet don't touch the charred ground,

will walk so her soft, blue feet
float above the tortured earth
and his incantatory
violence. He will watch her
reflections in broken glass,
but he will not meet her gaze.
He'll bow his head, stop his ears
against her, not having done
near enough to hear her name.

Hermes, Messenger of the Gods, God of Commerce and Theft, Purveyor of Souls to the Underworld, and God of Boundaries is Out of a Job; He Chain Smokes, Uses His Silver Helmet as an Ashtray, and Tries to Help a Visitor Negotiate the Door behind Which He's Locked

Try jiggling the handle. Sometimes that works . . . .

I'm not the go-to guy for picking locks,
but the doorknob--ingress, egress--that's all me.
It takes a middleman to valorize a need.
    The robocall, too. That was mine.
Put me out a job, though . . . inclined
folks to give me even less attention.
The hand truck, my latest invention--
the prototype was stolen by the faithful,
by definition a gateway crime.
                            Absolutely null
done after that. My higher ups don't call.
They don't. Nothing to deliver, dick all
else to do but wait for the phone to ring.
    Eternity's a bodark brier though the tongue;
it's waiting a callback for a starring role
in a spangly, new E.D. commercial.
I tend to tourists who think they've leverage
to cadge magic tricks. (Transmogrify gods
to chess pieces, or bop-a-clowns their fears inflate,
vacillate between worship, denigration,
and wonder why I'm out an occupation.
I'd ferry them to hell for a vacation.)
Got tired of demands, of being berated,
downgraded, good for only step and fetch.
It's the job, of course, but only if there's commerce
between the faithful--which they're not--and the gods,
which they maintain we aren't.
                            Beloved, I can only dumb
it down so much until the matter's zero / sum:
lacking one, the other's gone, a murder-suicide.
Can you prove you exist? The question's solipsistic:
A barista serves my order, and I believe
the taking doesn't prove she's given it to me,
while the paper cup burns my skin,

42

my nose snuffles black aroma in.
    There's more to you all than a couple of knocks.
Work me out. Sing to me of sorrows, loss,
I'll freight it on, faithful as a lover,
parrot it to all the gods I stumble over.

Laundry Day for Jesus and Synchronicity, Waggish
Roommates

Jesus unloads a washer
packed tight with his delicates—
rhinestone Nudie suits, lamé

pants--while Synchronicity
balls their vast array of socks
using an algorithm

on his tablet that will clock
out random beeps. He'll stop, take
the sock he's touching, and drop

it on the floor. Jesus makes
his way to the drier, loads
it up. He's no great shakes

at laundry, but all the clothes
somehow turn out perfectly.
Synchronicity helps fold,

fashioning a mad mare's nest
of clothes that never wrinkle,
rip, fade, or shrink. They work best

as a team. As though mingling,
Jesus climbs atop a chair
and goes all touchy feely.

He tells the meek he's sure they'll
get just what's coming to them.
As he did in Galilee,

his tone assumes a humming
lull rhyming with the driers.
Blessed are the merciful,

who'll always step on a rake . . . .
Jesus keeps them occupied,
while Synchronicity takes

his backpack, susses out loads
of whites in all the washers.
When no one's watching, he throws

in each, one red cotton sock.

Logophobia

Inside the bag, tongues babble, testing
the ruckused sky for gods. *Horse hoof. King snake.*
Red-tailed hawk. A tall, worn man tosses
the burlap sack into the truck bed, takes
another, walks to the shade tree where two men wait.

The word for which they search is not
Agkistrodon contortrix.
                    They'd call it
chunk head, death adder, white oak snake, Southern
copperhead, highland *or* dry-land moccasin,
poplar leaf, red oak, red snake. **Whatever
the word, they know** chapter and verse where it's found.
In summer, on limestone shelves heated by sunlight
or, in winter, crevasses—loved also
by timber rattlers. Sometimes, in fall,
on land swapped with the river or in leaf-bed,
they'll find it sunning, minding its own, awaiting
idiot mice.
            Whatever word they trust,
they still walk lightly, delicately
roust the next rock, test the next crevasse
for larger, fatter words. End of the day,
snake-rich and sweaty, they sing about the word
made flesh, undwelling among them.

Lord Jesus, let nothing unholy remain,
Apply Thine own blood and extract every stain;
To get this blest cleansing, I all things forego—
Now wash me, and I shall be whiter than snow.

One cries out words in an undulant, unknown
tongue, words none of them can spell, begins
a dance on the packed, rocky soil. The others
join, lifting hands, as on Sundays, when the word
they've gathered is spread on the floor, **alive**
and curving through stamping feet, taken up,
twining arms, necks, as the minister yells

. . . Getting back to the Sons of God. People say they're saved and sanctified. I'll tell you how much you're sanctified. As much of his word as you do, that's how much you're sanctified. The word will abide forever. You'll die on this earth, but that right there is going to abide forever.

The word abides as homesteads, razed, graded, paved,
become interchanges, off-ramps smelling
of deep fat and diesel. The word abides
as jobs they know to work leave for Bangladesh,
Sumatra, words they couldn't find on a map,
given a fat bag of chance and another
set of hands. The word abides as children
leave for Nashville, buy cowboy hats to wait on
people wearing cowboy hats. The word abides
because, alive in their hands, at their feet,
they take it up, some kissing the wedged,
metallic heads, some clasping them to breast.
A frowsy widow lifts aloft a copperhead,
fat, drowsy, as the dimmest of her sisters
lifts a rat-slack rattler, spins it around
like a nephew. A prom-shirted deacon
scream at both, leans into his screaming . . .

There'll be no more sufferin'-uh, there'll be no more sweat to wipe from the brow-uh, when we cross over the river Jordan-uh and we go home, and-uh . . . .

a three-piece band plays a rockabilly
drone, Chuck Berry fed through a chain saw,
and all are dancing, twirling, stamping,
weeping, lifting up whatever word
they use, as if God were floating over the church,
watching them, listening through the ceiling.

After a Career of Starring as the Corpse of People Blown Apart, Eaten by Sharks, and Mauled by the Living Dead, He's *Still* Got It

Outside Grauman's, he tripped, fell face first
into wet concrete, and stayed there five hours.
When the crowd thinned some, attendant workers
jack-hammered him free. He walked to his hearse,
got in, and drove off. No one thought too much
about it: after his *corpse run over*
by a Bush Hog, after *corpse imploding*
in a spaceship hurtling toward a black hole,
folk were harder to please. Still, they waited
for new work, new catastrophes.

He wakes at 5:00 a.m., still, calls his ex
to feel dead enough inside, and rises to start
his daily grind. Black coffee and burnt toast
with tar-pit marmalade. He hits the gym:
core work, free weights, treadmill to keep his weight
cadaverous. Afterwards, a shower.
Nine a.m., he's scheduling the day's shots:
corpse of self-immolated Buddhist monk
mauled by feral dogs; mime as corpse tartare
in a zombie buffet, the requisite
decapitations. He's pioneered four
different categories, myriad
subsections.
                    It's his craft: green screens, latex
maulery, chroma-key software, braces
for rigor mortis, his brilliant, grotesque
prosthetics, mindfulness meditation
to sustain his multi-million-dollar
death grimace.
                    Each scene pays ten thousand bucks:
corpse shot 14 times through a car windshield;
corpse of skydiver with necrotizing
fasciitis whose spare chute failed and who
was fished out of an active volcano.
He checks his database, tweaks, and invents.
Make-up, minutes posing, no editing—
by definition—uploading the shot.

He stays busy and doesn't read the trades.
He doesn't need scripts, answers inquiries
with *How did I die?* He shoots some fifty,
sixty scenes a week.
                            He's only done one
promotional tour. Dragged on stage and heaped
in the spotlight, he refused to answer
questions, humiliated the emcee.
    You'd call him lucky at the start--chosen
from a cattle call, he made the casting
director *believe* he was dead even
as he read the scene, contorted thusly.
After that first role, there were dues to pay:
screen guild wages, chump bit parts--*stumped remains
of gator frenzy; rotted Nazi ten.*
Then, his big break: on an autopsy slab
five hours straight, he remained in character
when the dimmest son of the prop master
thought he was a mannequin. Dragging him
to the warehouse, the boy stopped for a smoke,
struck a match on his face. Powers that be
notice things like that. Focus groups *believed*
he was dead. Protestors castigated
studios for mutilating corpses.
The suits were smart enough to keep quiet,
a plausible deniability.
He issued no disclaimer and kept low,
developing his database, working
at his art: *sunbaked corpse in a life raft,
gull savaged;* various asphyxias
(auto-erotic, carbon monoxide);
*airplane crash survivor eaten alive
by ex-girlfriend.*
                            Offers rained down on him
when focus groups found the same film better
with him than without, bumped the bottom line
(deride the profit motive as you will)
the breadth of a death rattle. His seconds
on screen (*corpse of a Black Friday shopper;
radiation victim found, rat-ravaged,
in a dumpster*) left the toughest critic
gasping for breath.

He could have marketed
bottled water or an exercise craze.
If someone wrote the *Mr. Death Diet*,
it would have made *The New York Times Book Review*
He gave it all up for death, perfection
of his gruesome craft: *drowning victim sucked*
through industrial desalinator;
corpse digested, disgorged by Great White shark
and peeled from UV overexposure.
This last, a public service announcement:

"Nine out of ten dermatologists say:
'Sun block . . . . Use it! Whatever else happens,
no one wants to leave a leathery stiff.'"

He keeps a low profile, avoiding fans,
inventing deaths not thought about for films
not yet proposed.
                        If he goes out, he walks,
hat pulled low. He gave up on autographs
years ago, but wannabes surround him.
Some drop to the sidewalk when they see him
gliding along. They give him their head shots.
They give him contortions—*corpse of a man*
under a piano dropped five stories;
man run over by clown-driven jet trolley.
Some call him out, dumb, plebian mimics
of his salad days--tributes not clever,
though one dismemberment, he had to stop
and think about. They give him resumes.
He takes them, does nothing, seeing nothing
he has to offer.
                        These days, he's seldom
seen in public. Some say he phones roles in,
but he's never been in greater demand.
Perky, young actresses, sylphs with rocket
trajectories, have turned down starring roles
when his is not the suppurating corpse
found beneath the stairs, tucked in nuptial beds,
stowed in the trunk of step-dad's Caddy,
his contortions, impossible, his face,
always a rictus of off-screen horror.

Coyote

The night before my 68th, I dreamed

of walking a bookmarked scrap of land.

I saw a coyote following me.

He wasn't threatening, just staring,

just sizing me up. I didn't want to

be sized up. I walked the other direction.

He followed, ran to me, heeled.

We walked together.

I ignored him. He stayed heeled.

We came to an abandoned stable, walked in.

I stopped in front of a stall.

The coyote climbed up the door,

arced his body across the gap, gracefully draped himself

       across my shoulders.

I stood there, not wanting to move, the coyote

snugged against me. Maybe I worried

about fleas. Maybe I was guarding his sleep.

I don't know how long I was still and quiet.

I don't know

how time is measured there.

Part 4: Yes and No and Yes . . . .

Between Sunday School and Church, Just Prior to Their First Communion, Pre-Teens of First Baptist Church, Wakinsville, Georgia, Slide Down the Grassy Slopes of an Excavation That Was Expected to Fill with Rain Water and Become a Pond, but Never Did Either

They have no language for what they all become.
Sunday School notwithstanding, there's no language
for their slidings. Church clothes change to gravestone rubbings,

stained by red clay, grass, detritus plenicolor.
Darwin in abeyance, they're fish by the bottom,
beyond instruction or parental admonition.

They dream fish dreams of tractable ooze, deep weeds, light
streaming, chiaroscuro, from the surface, while down
deeper, gathered round a dead aerator, catfish,

pike, alligator gar imagine cut banks, oxbow
lakes, the privacy of first cigarettes, darkness
presaging lightning strikes at dim fry in the shallows,

stirred silt, the violence, satisfactions
separate and singular. But parents tempt
with donuts, attendance stickers. Coaxed up the bank,

their reds, greens, fade beneath the hands of spit-shining
moms, pant-dusting, impatient dads. They shrug against
improvement, slouch audacity. They fidget with

their families throughout the service, awaiting
their first communion. The body and blood of Christ,
they're told, these splashes of grape juice, these stale crackers.

Not enough. They can't say how they know, but they must,
that such is a greyhound's rabbit, an edging, not
the downward slide into the dark miraculous.

Against the Possibility of Odd or Sloppy Expressions of Grief, the City of Dahlonega, Georgia, Erects a Sign at the Entrance of a Municipal Cemetery That Says CITY NOT RESPONSIBLE FOR ITEMS LEFT ON GRAVES

Maybe someone brought a tennis racket,
lost it, and didn't think, until a match,
where she'd spotted it last: in bas-relief
with the headstone. She'd left it, distracted
by grief, but returned, nagged groundsmen ragged.

Here, the city wants homogenized grief,
funereal wildness subsumed beneath
the neat, green lawn, kept graves, white headstones ranked
and mapped for reference. Any beliefs,
displays foreign to municipal chiefs

will be ignored, uncollected--frankly,
will be seen as maligning the dead, dank
unmourned anymore. How did such a sign
become a needful thing? Did sextons tank
their keeping up, collecting thanklessly

benighted tokens? Did walking a line,
grave to sullen grave, become one long whine
of dodging detritus, wine bottles, beer
cans, love-wreckage, dead flowers, all the things
prompting municipal actions to bring

order to grief's savagery?
                            We see, here,
the dull result, an ennui without peer.
But drafts of the sign (the unselected
specifics considered, then disappeared)
might clarify the city fathers' fears:

NO PROSTRATE WIDOWS WILL BE COLLECTED.
ALL GRAVES AFTER DARK WILL BE PROTECTED
BY FERAL DOGS.
                    NO SUSPECT REVELRY.

Drafts rejected, the precept selected,
fabricated, finally erected

consolidates intentions handily,
encapsulates a city policy
subtle as a genital infection:
Your losses mean dick-all to us, so see
that you let seem be finale of be.

The antiseptic message selected
voted on, the signage, disinfected,
placed at the main gate's entrance, cast no pall,
kept the graveyard dull, its bleak objective.
One more absurdity to genuflect.

I want to uproot the sign at night, haul
it through the graveyard. I'll select, withal,
a grave at random, the most neglected, say,
and dig a hole deep enough to install
the sign to test the letter of the law,

to show what's said that nothing said can stay.

Pantoum, a Raging Oxymoron: The Parents of an Ex-Student Who Died of an Overdose Commemorate Him by Planting a Dogwood Tree, Which Lives for Eighty Years—and Seems an Odd Investment—to Memorialize His Full-Stop Nineteen or So

A dogwood blooms above a brazen plaque,
remembrance of a student dead of oxy.
Planted by his parents, I guess, the act
seems starkly out of step with orthodoxy:

commemorate a young man dead of oxy,
we commemorate a graceless lie,
an outrage to the orthodoxy.
We celebrate the ageless lives—to die

from self-indulgence is a graceless lie
implicit in any such remembrance.
We celebrate the ageless lives well lived—to die
so stupidly implies a severance.

Implicit in any such remembrance
are all our aspirations undermined
stupidly—remembrance of severance,
the oxymoron, perfectly defined.

Are aspirations also undermined
by overkill? Decades of dogwood blooms
(an oxymoron, perfectly defined)
for a kid who tossed his life assuming

his longevity. Ditch the dogwood blooms.
Sow annuals: a yearly replanting
for a kid who tossed his life, a resuming
of grief-work every spring, recanting

perpetuity by yearly replanting
their loss. Short lives rate short-term statements,
redundant spring grief-work, a recanting
of a faith beyond ironic debasement

of their loss. Short lives rate short-term statements,
not pantomimes of hollow, tacky hope,

of faith beyond ironic debasement,
remembrance of a life pissed up a rope.

A pantomime, a hollow, tacky hope,
this dogwood blooming above a brazen plaque,
remembrance of a life pissed up a rope.
His was not a life that blooming re-enacts.

Villanelle: Non-Being and Real Estate

I live in a place named after a place--
no cove or foxes on "Fox Cove."
In selling what's not, or has been erased,

however fantastically contrived, the name--
"Railroad Esplanade," "Magnolia Oaks Road"—
just seems a place named after a place

and only suggests a modicum of grace
mortgaged and inhabited, not bestowed.
This selling what's not, or has been erased--

see "Happy Valley" and "Victory Estates"--
provokes a spinal question. What do I prove
when I live in a place named after a place?

Terrain of pseudonyms, a way to face
the no one left to be, the nowhere left to go
when we live in a place named after a place,
when we've bought what's not, what's been erased.

Questions Arise when I See Buzzards Circling a Day Care Center and Remember That, in Flight, They're Called a "Kettle"

A shell game gliding the thermals,
circling slowly to sucker the rubes:
Come closer, Cuz . . . I got sump'n
to show you. Passing, I hope
it's the dumpster, its aggregate
of soiled didies, ripening
in soupy Georgia heat.

Why a kettle?

For how they swirl, a stew stirred
to a centripetal vortex,
fixing, at the bottom,
an iota of meat?

And the children who dig in the sand
and never think of burial,

if not too short to look up,
do they recall the mobiles that taught
them what's beyond their reach?

Do they await a dirt angel
the lowest will make when it smacks
the playground's epicenter oak?

And one, apart from the rest, pushes
the merry-go-round to a gallop,
hops on and, holding the rails, leans back,
eyes closed for the whirling dark, testing

what it's like to float.

Sonnet with Cheese, No Mayo: At a Burger Joint Drive-Through, I Remember a Rookie Calf, Running & Kicking & Being an Ass

I saw, driving home from work, a pasture
on the right. I saw among the placid,
grazing herd, anomalous, a manic
calf, not two ticks older than yesterday,

start up from wary, experimental
grazing and, at a broken-field run, kick
at air, kick sideways at the principle
of standing still again. God bless his slick,

pristine ignorance of a future writ
in hamburger, how his fluttering hooves
will fuel creeping toward the take-out window
and measuring my life by car lengths moved.

While offering him our requiescat,
I tell the server *No.*
                    No fries with that.

At a Stoplight in August, Quitting Time & All of Watkinsville Catches the Same Light, Heats the New Road's Asphalt with Exhaust and Gunned Motors

I turned off the radio, the AC, to watch a hawk
sifting the sky, the ground. He saw movement,
dropped like a white-hot hammer.

A tussle, weed witnessed, and the hawk rose, a lament
gaining altitude, slowly, the attendant circling.
I saw, finally, the rat. He ran to the curb, hesitant,

took a solid beat before jumping,
began an up-tempo buck & wing on the molten asphalt,
a spate of grands jetés under and among waiting

cars, trucks, the hawk swooping low to assess the gestalt
beneath him. He never stopped floating,
but didn't drop, pinned as he was to the cobalt.

I told my friend Mary, and Mary reported
how the rat wasn't dancing, how his feet nose vibrations,
how the skin there, thinner than an ex-wife's, sorts

dark intentions. She gave me documentation,
but I don't care about rats' feet, generally.
Hawks' wings, yes, for they soar above commotion.

So boiling the event to a speck, what I'll keep
is the frantic rat bopping the hot pavement.
It makes me grin and makes me resent

what Mary said about membranes, changing habitat,
ecological specialization. It's too much
to evaluate. I'd rather believe in dancing rats.

Anybody would. That's just common sense.

A Dog's Job of Work (Brisa, Hank, requiescat in pace)

Having taken the front yard, the trees almost to their summits,
English ivy snakes, interweaves, tunnels down beneath deadfall,
leaf rot, a rake left out last spring, emerges as Gordian
tangles, strands too brittle for half tugs. Against such folderol

Hank's élan, grabbing rag ends from my hand, tugging strands to
ground, wrangling, berserk, and digging straight down for roots. I
praise the dog, his job of work, this deconstruction of knot, snarl,
and tangle. Above all not sorted, he hovers, hikes his leg, zings,

negates offending particulars on trash cans, tires, any smaller
dog--oracular, sure-fire, his eponymous persistence.
He attends. Where Maggie pisses, he sniffs and pisses the same
to show newcomers how thoroughly she's lied, how history

and process end at his decrial--methodologies, creeds,
professions, empiricists' smug bastions, metaphysics, all
met with his stream. Irrefutable, fluid as a hot God's
judgment, his nose for consequence, dissemblance, remedy, fraud.

Dog, keep me from intention, baffle, rote, from yearning, yearly
subscription to *Better Homes and Gardens.* Teach me the wrangle
and growl, the subjugating snarlings, tangles, unrakeable
and libertine, to asymmetrical cunning—the manglings

and tumblings requisite to howl against geometrical
containment. Rage at receptacles—cardboard boxes' hubris,
smug logos' filagree, all gnawed, soaked, worried down to wilting.
Demonstrate, I pray, the height, breadth, and depth of damn-fool

daring, discernment, the knack for unaccepting unsniffed evidence,
and all proofs unbitten and unbatted. Provide such ferule
as channels energies of nose, teeth, claw, and tear, your purview.
Share with me your verve. Deliver me from the Levitical.

Ideal Reader: Poem for My Daughter

Sarah decides, casting about for a tattoo,
on lines in a poem I wrote for her: *We want*
a pebble's worth of riot. Footsteps on the moon.

She gets it tattooed on her right foot, wears sandals
to her job bartending. It's summer. Co-workers
see the tat, want to see the poem. Sarah gives
them copies. Each picks a line, an image, goes
to the same tattoo parlor. Cooings and envy
abound as friends—and their friends' various buddies--
ask to see my manuscript, which they savage
into sentences, phrases, nouns, modifiers,
verbs, clauses adjectival *and* adverbial.

Expressions contort their ways through cognoscenti,
hangers on, denizens of the cultural blip.
Screeds, inked in swirly fonts. Freight their feet will carry
the rest of their lives. One by one, then rivulets
at a time, they troop downtown, armed with a trenchant
image, a planed phrase, verses blooming on their feet.

Anonymous decades become a demitasse
of ink, festoon ankles, soles, tops of feet, calves, toes,
slither from a tendon toward a heel.
Summer comes again; it's almost salmonesque,
the way they head up town, over the wheeling
weeks, to the same boutique. The same, tired shoe salesman
waits on all of them. Hundreds he waits on, reading
their feet, taking in my manuscript,
no titles, no sequence. Just ink and more women
coming, hundreds. He's reading. He's never read this much . . . .

The lines, images coalesce the way a drop
of water takes in another, polarities
aligning, volume increasing surface pressure.
Another drop assimilated. More pressure.
No telling where the rupture will occur. No telling . . . .

Anyhow, weeks later, I'm out window shopping,
thinking leathers, prices, stitching, heels, and he steps
into sunlight, squinting, walks the block with me, quiet
at first. Then, fidgeting, almost hang-dogged, he says,
"I need to shake your hand. I'm damned if I know why."

Villanelle: When My Youngest Son Was Coming to Terms with Gravity, He Would *Not* Be Instructed

Success had made you fearless, and you laughed,
though there was a floor beneath your leaping bliss,
and good faith steps will sometimes bust your ass.

You climbed on last night's sofa bed, amassed
your vertical skills, and toddled to its precipice.
Success had made you fearless, and you laughed;

then took the hand's breadth drop into the massed
and tousled pallet too sprawling for a near miss
or good faith steps that turn to bust your ass.

I hope for you, bold son, eternally vast
indifference to a possible concrete kiss—
that success will hold you fearless, and you'll laugh

through infinite soft landings, when odds are cast
against your free-stepping hubris
and good faith steps sneak round to bust your ass.

It will not be so—the hope contrasts
with what I know of leaping, making me remiss:
Success will make you fearless, and you'll laugh
as good faith steps rush round to bust your ass.

**Long Beers after Settling in: A Bird Bath for the New House
(a poem for my wife)**

A fall-fat robin waits on its rim,
framed by trees I can name, shrubs I can't.
I catch his eye. Casually, we bow and drink,
bow and drink, bow and drink, an homage
to she who argued, chose, bought,
lugged, placed, and filled it.
I do my part and say *You're welcome,*
for her sake, at every sip he takes,
I take, he takes, I take.

Feeder

Scrabbling colors--birds rioting seed,
a broadcast punctuated
by squirrels
          as I hand feeders
from limbs, rails, poles, to my short wife.
She fills them, hands them back,
a Saturday task done
for luck, for variegated finches;
dull republican sparrows; blue jays,
braying fundamentalists; and,
this morning, one bald cardinal—
alopecia or a mate's black
savagery.
         The morning rhymes
with dirt-roads, years arranging,
rearranging the evenings' crows'
F'koff! F'koff! or hearing one night, two cold
stanzas into a poem that gave me only
two, a fluttering, then silence quilting
the beat before the rasping, bitter
call of the existentialist bird,
pure pique drawn naked
over a cheese grater.
           It cried once,
flew away, never returned,
or at least, I never heard it.
But there's a resonance, even now,
something in me saying *Yes . . . yes, you're right.*

Sometimes, it's just like that.

Not for what we offer, birds come,
not because not offering would keep them
here or away.
         Small charities suggest,
suggest, suggest, suggest, each repetition
feting the air thicker, stubbing any move
against an ignorant amazement
that isn't anything but a lack
of anything else.

Once, Fort Worth, I saw deke birds fall
from St. Patrick's cathedral. Conical lumps
sprouted wings, veered upward inches from smash,
worked air to gabled roof peak
for yet another hurling.
                    They didn't feed as they fell,
weren't gaudy about it, weren't attracting mates.

The plunge was itself, the rushing down,
wings clamped to succor a plummet
so intense it seemed a longing,
a sidewalk smack avoided
by a feather's breadth.
                    Dropping,
they sang, their cry, a large tear
drawn upward through a slide whistle.

I don't know all the birds outside
our window, don't want to know,
don't know why, but we feed them,
not for what's done, but that they've come,
that they're here, and we know as much.

It's not so much a hoping
as a way of living in lieu of. We do;
they come. They'd come, anyway,
but in our doing, we welcome
the scrabbling wings, the hunger
toward which we raise our hands.

Acknowledgements:

My profound appreciation for the kindness, insight, and skepticism of several friends who helped in assembling this manuscript: Marisa Pagnattaro, Molly Hodges, Terry Easton, Hugh Ruppersburg, Derek Thiess, Laura Ng, B.J. Robinson, and Don and Susan Wells. My special thanks to Alan Abrams, editor of Sligo Creek Publishing, for his efforts in taking this project to completion.

Several of these poems have appeared previously in journals and periodicals. "Husbandry" appeared in the newsletter of the Jung Society of Atlanta, "Non-Being and Real Estate" in *Better than Starbucks*, "In a Sudden Downpour at a Poorly Planned Blues Festival, The Ghost of Robert Johnson Comes Upon a Dumpy Guy Sitting in the Rain on a Wooden Crate & Eating A Soggy Sparerib Sandwich" appeared in *Poetry Quarterly*, "Long Beers after Settling In" appeared in *The Lullwater Review*, "Leavening" appeared in *The Scarlet Leaf Review*, and "Poem for Uncle Jackass" and "When a Woman's Finally Had Enough in Alligator, Mississippi, She Walks Down Highway 61 to 444, Doglegs To Highway One, Turns South, and Walks to Rosedale" appeared in *The Arkansas Review;* "Just as a Huge Tree Falls into Minnesota's Lake Itaska and Begins Its Drift Southward on the Mississippi, an Underwater Welder Talks to me about Diving, Zero Visibility, and the Threat Imposed by Neutral Buoyancy (Greenville, Mississippi)" and "After an Impossibly Steep Hill in Yazoo City, through Three Stoplights, Past Where Wu Hor's Grocery Use to Be, Then over the Humped-Up Railroad Crossing . . . " appeared in *Delta Poetry Review*.

www.ingramcontent.com/pod-product-compliance
Lightning Source LLC
Chambersburg PA
CBHW071541120626
46550CB00006B/2536